cakes
& treats

betty saw

cakes
& treats

betty saw

Marshall Cavendish
Cuisine

Designer: Benson Tan
Series Designer: Bernard Go Kwang Meng

Copyright © 2008 Marshall Cavendish International (Asia) Private Limited
Reprinted 2009, 2010

Published by Marshall Cavendish Cuisine
An imprint of Marshall Cavendish International
1 New Industrial Road, Singapore 536196

Other Marshall Cavendish Offices:
Marshall Cavendish International. PO Box 65829 London EC1P 1NY, UK • Marshall Cavendish Corporation. 99 White Plains Road, Tarrytown NY 10591-9001, USA • Marshall Cavendish International (Thailand) Co Ltd. 253 Asoke, 12th Flr, Sukhumvit 21 Road, Klongtoey Nua, Wattana, Bangkok 10110, Thailand • Marshall Cavendish (Malaysia) Sdn Bhd, Times Subang, Lot 46, Subang Hi-Tech Industrial Park, Batu Tiga, 40000 Shah Alam, Selangor Darul Ehsan, Malaysia

Marshall Cavendish is a trademark of Times Publishing Limited

National Library Board Singapore Cataloguing in Publication Data

Saw, Betty.
Cakes & treats / Betty Saw. – Singapore : Marshall Cavendish Cuisine, c2008.
p. cm. – (Mini cookbooks)
ISBN-13 : 978-981-261-582-4
ISBN-10 : 981-261-582-2

1. Cake. 2. Snack foods. I. Title. II. Series: Mini cookbooks

TX771
641.8653 -- dc22   OCN213361209

Printed in Malaysia by Times Offset (M) Sdn Bhd

banana fritters Makes about 40

This recipe offers a delicious way to use up ripe bananas.

INGREDIENTS

Self-raising flour	120 g ($4^{1}/_{2}$ oz)
Corn flour (cornstarch)	30 g (1 oz)
Baking powder	1 tsp
Salt	$^{1}/_{4}$ tsp
Eggs	2
Sugar	30 g (1 oz)
Coconut milk	125 ml (4 fl oz / $^{1}/_{2}$ cup), obtained from squeezing $^{1}/_{2}$ grated coconut mixed with sufficient water
Ripe bananas (*rastali* variety)	5, medium, peeled and mashed
Cooking oil for deep-frying	

METHOD

- Sift both types of flour and baking powder together into a mixing bowl. Add salt.

- Whisk eggs and sugar until light and fluffy. Fold in sifted ingredients alternately with coconut milk.

- Add mashed bananas and mix well.

- Heat oil in a wok. Drop tablespoonfuls of batter into hot oil and fry until golden brown. Do this in batches. Drain well before serving.

weights and measures

Quantities for this book are given in Metric, Imperial and American (spoon and cup) measures. Standard spoon and cup measurements used are: 1 tsp = 5 ml, 1 Tbsp = 15 ml, 1 cup = 250 ml. All measures are level unless otherwise stated.

Liquid And Volume Measures

Metric	Imperial	American
5 ml	$1/6$ fl oz	1 teaspoon
10 ml	$1/3$ fl oz	1 dessertspoon
15 ml	$1/2$ fl oz	1 tablespoon
60 ml	2 fl oz	$1/4$ cup (4 tablespoons)
85 ml	$2 1/2$ fl oz	$1/3$ cup
90 ml	3 fl oz	$3/8$ cup (6 tablespoons)
125 ml	4 fl oz	$1/2$ cup
180 ml	6 fl oz	$3/4$ cup
250 ml	8 fl oz	1 cup
300 ml	10 fl oz ($1/2$ pint)	$1 1/4$ cups
375 ml	12 fl oz	$1 1/2$ cups
435 ml	14 fl oz	$1 3/4$ cups
500 ml	16 fl oz	2 cups
625 ml	20 fl oz (1 pint)	$2 1/2$ cups
750 ml	24 fl oz ($1 1/5$ pints)	3 cups
1 litre	32 fl oz ($1 3/5$ pints)	4 cups
1.25 litres	40 fl oz (2 pints)	5 cups
1.5 litres	48 fl oz ($2 2/5$ pints)	6 cups
2.5 litres	80 fl oz (4 pints)	10 cups

Dry Measures

Metric	Imperial
30 grams	1 ounce
45 grams	$1 1/2$ ounces
55 grams	2 ounces
70 grams	$2 1/2$ ounces
85 grams	3 ounces
100 grams	$3 1/2$ ounces
110 grams	4 ounces
125 grams	$4 1/2$ ounces
140 grams	5 ounces
280 grams	10 ounces
450 grams	16 ounces (1 pound)
500 grams	1 pound, $1 1/2$ ounces
700 grams	$1 1/2$ pounds
800 grams	$1 3/4$ pounds
1 kilogram	2 pounds, 3 ounces
1.5 kilograms	3 pounds, $4 1/2$ ounces
2 kilograms	4 pounds, 6 ounces

Oven Temperature

	°C	°F	Gas Regulo
Very slow	120	250	1
Slow	150	300	2
Moderately slow	160	325	3
Moderate	180	350	4
Moderately hot	190/200	375/400	5/6
Hot	210/220	410/425	6/7
Very hot	230	450	8
Super hot	250/290	475/550	9/10

Length

Metric	Imperial
0.5 cm	$1/4$ inch
1 cm	$1/2$ inch
1.5 cm	$3/4$ inch
2.5 cm	1 inch

Abbreviation

tsp	teaspoon
Tbsp	tablespoon
g	gram
kg	kilogram
ml	millilitre

contents

cakes & treats

pineapple upside-down cake

Makes one 22-cm (9-in) square cake

This cake was popular back in the 1950s in America. It has a moist texture and the pineapple rings and cherries make it look very pretty.

INGREDIENTS

Pineapple rings	9
Maraschino cherries	5, halved
Cold butter	250 g (9 oz), diced
Castor (superfine) sugar	225 g (8 oz)
Eggs	4, large
Vanilla essence	1 tsp
Self-raising flour	240 g ($8^{1}/_{2}$ oz)
Pineapple juice	1–2 Tbsp

PINEAPPLE CREAM

Cold butter	250 g (9 oz), diced
Icing sugar	150 g ($5^{1}/_{3}$ oz), sifted
Vanilla essence	1 tsp
Evaporated milk	175 ml (6 fl oz), chilled
Pineapple juice	2 Tbsp, chilled

METHOD

• Line a 22-cm (9-in) square cake tin with greaseproof paper. Grease paper, then arrange pineapple rings in 3 rows of 3 to cover base of tin. Place a cherry half in the centre of each ring.

• Cream butter and sugar until light and creamy. Add eggs one at a time and beat until incorporated. Add vanilla essence. Sift in half the flour and fold into mixture. Repeat with remaining half of flour. Add pineapple juice to achieve soft, dropping consistency.

• Carefully spread batter over top of pineapple rings. Bake in a preheated 175°C (350°F) oven for 40–45 minutes, or until a skewer inserted into the centre of cake comes out clean. Turn out and leave to cool on a wire rack.

- Meanwhile, prepare pineapple cream. Beat butter with sugar until light and creamy. Add vanilla essence, then beat in milk a little at a time until incorporated. Beat in pineapple juice.

- Decorate cake as desired with pineapple cream.

apple cake
Makes one 22-cm (9-in) square cake

A light and simple cake with a layer of cinnamon-coated apple for an extra special touch.

INGREDIENTS

Brown sugar	2–3 Tbsp
Plain (all-purpose) flour (A)	2 Tbsp, sifted
Ground cinnamon	2 tsp
Apples	4, peeled and cored, then thinly and evenly sliced
Eggs	4, large
Castor (superfine) sugar	225 g (8 oz)
Corn oil	250 ml (8 fl oz / 1 cup)
Vanilla essence	1 tsp
Salt	1 pinch
Cold water	150–180 ml (5–6 fl oz)
Plain (all-purpose) flour (B)	300 g (11 oz)
Baking powder	2 tsp

METHOD

- Line a 22-cm (9-in) square cake tin with greaseproof paper. Grease paper and set aside.

- Combine brown sugar, flour (A) and cinnamon in a bowl. Add apple slices and toss to coat. Set aside.

- Whisk eggs and sugar. Add corn oil, vanilla essence, salt and water. Sift in flour (B) and baking powder.

- Pour half the batter into prepared tin. Arrange apple slices on top, then spread remaining batter over apple slices to barely cover them. It does not matter if slices stick out.

- Bake in a preheated 175°C (350°F) oven for 45–60 minutes. Turn out and leave to cool on a wire rack.

apple cheesecake Makes one 21-cm (8.5-cm) cake

This is a lovely combination of light sponge cake and baked cheesecake topped with a tangy-sweet layer of baked apples.

INGREDIENTS

Brown sugar	75 g (2$^1/_2$ oz)
Ground cinnamon	$^1/_2$ tsp
Red apples	3, medium, peeled and cored, then thinly and evenly sliced
Plain (all-purpose) flour	150 g (5$^1/_3$ oz)
Baking powder	1 tsp
Sugar	115 g (4 oz)
Eggs	2
Corn oil	115 ml (3$^2/_3$ fl oz)
Vanilla essence	$^1/_2$ tsp
Salt	1 pinch

CHEESE LAYER

Cream cheese	250 g (9 oz), softened at room temperature
Sugar	55 g (2 oz)
Egg	1
Vanilla essence	$^1/_2$ tsp

METHOD

- Prepare cheese layer. Beat cream cheese until smooth, then add sugar and beat until creamy. Add egg and vanilla essence and beat until smooth.

- Grease a 21-cm (8$^1/_2$-in) round springform cake tin.

- Combine brown sugar and cinnamon in a bowl. Add apple slices and toss to coat. Set aside.

- Sift flour and baking powder together. Set aside.

- Beat sugar and eggs. Add corn oil and vanilla essence and beat well. Add sifted ingredients and salt.

- Spread batter evenly in prepared cake tin. Bake in a preheated 175°C (350°F) oven for 15 minutes.

- Remove cake from oven. Quickly spoon cheese layer over and arrange apple slices over cheese. Return cake to oven and bake for another 35–40 minutes.

- Remove cake from tin and leave to cool before serving.

indonesian layer cake Makes one 17-cm (7-in) square cake

This lovely spice cake is commonly known as *kek lapis* in Singapore, Malaysia and Indonesia.

INGREDIENTS

Eggs	7, yolks and whites separated
Sugar	150 g (5^1/$_3$ oz)
Vanilla essence	1 tsp
Butter	150 g (5^1/$_3$ oz), softened at room temperature, then beaten
Brandy	1 Tbsp
Plain (all-purpose) flour	90 g (3^1/$_3$ oz), sifted
Mixed spice	^{1}/$_4$ tsp, sifted

METHOD

• Grease base and sides of a 17-cm (7-in) square cake tin. Line base with greaseproof paper and grease paper. Set aside.

• Whisk eggs yolks, sugar and vanilla essence until creamy. Beat in butter and brandy. Stir in sifted ingredients. Set aside.

• Whisk eggs whites until just stiff. Pour egg-yolk mixture over beaten egg whites. Fold gently.

• Place prepared cake tin under a preheated grill for 1 minute. Remove from grill and add a ladleful of batter. Spread batter evenly by rolling your wrist to tilt tin. Return cake tin to grill for 5 minutes, or until batter is lightly brown. Repeat to layer and grill batter until batter is used up.

• Turn cake out and leave to cool on a wire rack.

pear cake Makes one 20-cm (8-in) round cake

This wonderfully moist cake can be made using any type of pear. It is ideal with a cup of tea.

INGREDIENTS

Plain (all-purpose) flour	180 g (6^1/$_2$ oz)
Baking powder	1 tsp
Pear	1, medium–large, peeled and cored, then thinly and evenly sliced
Brown sugar	210 g (7^1/$_2$ oz) + more for topping (optional)
Butter	180 g (6^1/$_2$ oz)
Eggs	2
Brandy	2 Tbsp

METHOD

• Line a 20-cm (8-in) round cake tin with greaseproof paper. Grease paper and set aside.

• Sift flour and baking powder together. Set aside.

• Toss pear slices in 60 g (2^1/$_4$ oz) brown sugar. Set aside.

• Cream butter and remaining brown sugar until light and fluffy. Add eggs one at a time, beating well after each addition. Fold in sifted ingredients together with brandy.

• Spread batter in prepared cake tin evenly. Arrange pear slices on surface of batter. Bake in a preheated 175°C (350°F) oven for 50 minutes.

• Remove cake from oven and sprinkle some brown sugar over the top while still hot, if desired.

carrot cake Makes one 22-cm (9-in) square cake

Lightly flavoured with ground cinnamon and packed with nuts, this moist carrot cake is a real treat. Use any type of nut as desired.

INGREDIENTS

Castor (superfine) sugar	225 g (8 oz)
Corn oil	250 ml (8 fl oz / 1 cup)
Eggs	3, large
Plain (all-purpose) flour	150 g (5$^1/_3$ oz)
Baking powder	1$^1/_2$ tsp
Bicarbonate of soda	1$^1/_3$ tsp
Ground cinnamon	1$^1/_3$ tsp
Salt	$^1/_2$ tsp
Carrot	250 g (9 oz), peeled and grated
Chopped nuts	125 g (4$^1/_2$ oz)

METHOD

- Line a 22-cm (9-in) square cake tin with greaseproof paper. Grease paper and set aside.

- Beat sugar in corn oil, then beat in eggs one at a time. Sift in flour, baking powder, bicarbonate of soda, cinnamon and salt, then fold into mixture. Stir in grated carrot and chopped nuts.

- Pour batter into prepared tin. Bake in a preheated 165°C (325°F) oven for about 45 minutes, or until a skewer inserted into the centre of cake comes out clean.

peach custard sandwich cake

Sandwiched and covered with bright yellow custard, this cake offers an alternative to the more common cream cakes.

INGREDIENTS

Corn oil	1 Tbsp
Rum	1 Tbsp
Peach syrup	2 Tbsp
Eggs	4, large
Castor (superfine) sugar	110 g (4 oz)
Self-raising flour	120 g ($4^1/_2$ oz), sifted
Canned sliced peaches	1 can (870 g / 1 lb $14^1/_2$ oz)

CUSTARD CREAM

Corn flour (cornstarch)	40 g ($1^1/_2$ oz)
Custard powder	40 g ($1^1/_2$ oz)
Milk	565 ml (19 fl oz)
Sugar	110 g (4 oz)
Butter	45 g ($1^1/_2$ oz)
Egg	1, well beaten
Vanilla essence	1 tsp
Peach syrup	1 Tbsp
Rum	1 Tbsp

METHOD

• Prepare custard cream. Blend corn flour, custard powder and 115 ml (4 fl oz) milk. Set aside. Bring remaining milk, sugar and butter to the boil in a saucepan. Add blended mixture, stirring constantly until mixture thickens. Remove from heat, then beat in egg, vanilla essence, peach syrup and rum. Set aside.

• Combine corn oil, rum and 1 Tbsp syrup. Set aside.

• Whisk eggs and sugar until light and fluffy. Sift in flour and fold quickly. Stir in corn-oil mixture.

- Line two 18 x 27-cm (7 x 11-in) cake tins with greaseproof paper. Grease paper. Divide batter equally between tins. Bake in a preheated 175°C (350°F) oven for 10–15 minutes, or until tops are golden. Drizzle remaining syrup over cakes.

- Sandwich custard cream between cakes. Spread cream over top and sides of cake sandwich as desired. Arrange peach slices decoratively on cake. If preferred, cake can be served chilled.

crunchy-top cake
Makes one 20-cm (8-in) round cake

The crunchy layer of sugar and the refreshing flavour from the lemon and orange zest in the cake make this a winner especially with children.

INGREDIENTS

Butter	250 g (9 oz)
Castor (superfine) sugar	210 g (7$\frac{1}{2}$ oz)
Orange zest	grated from 1 orange
Lemon zest	grated from 1 lemon
Eggs	4, large
Self-raising flour	240 g (8$\frac{1}{2}$ oz)
Orange juice or milk	1 Tbsp
Demerara sugar	60 g (2$\frac{1}{4}$ oz)
Sugar	1 Tbsp

METHOD

- Line a 20-cm (8-in) round cake tin with greaseproof paper. Grease paper and set aside.

- Cream butter and sugar until light and fluffy. Add orange and lemon zest. Add eggs one at a time, beating well after each addition. Sift in half the flour, then stir. Repeat with other half. Stir in orange juice or milk.

- Spoon batter into prepared tin. Even out surface. Bake on centre shelf in a preheated 175°C (350°F) oven for 25 minutes.

- Without removing cake from oven, sprinkle demerara sugar over the top. Bake for another 15 minutes, or until cake is done. To test, a skewer inserted into the centre of cake should come out clean.

dreamy cheesecake Makes a 21-cm (8¹/₂-in) round cake

The thin layer of cream cheese is just enough to whet the appetite, without it being too cloying or rich.

INGREDIENTS

Butter	180 g (6¹/₂ oz)
Icing sugar	150 g (5¹/₃ oz), sifted
Vanilla essence	¹/₂ tsp
Egg yolks	2
Egg white	1
Self-raising flour	150 g (5¹/₃ oz), sifted
Cold water	75 ml (2¹/₂ fl oz)
Melted chocolate (optional)	

CHEESE LAYER

Cream cheese	250 g (9 oz), softened at room temperature
Egg yolks	2
Castor (superfine) sugar	4 Tbsp
Vanilla essence	1 tsp
Lemon essence	1 tsp
Egg whites	4

METHOD

- Prepare cheese layer. Beat cream cheese until smooth, then add egg yolks one at a time until incorporated. Beat in sugar and essences. Set aside. Whisk egg whites until soft peaks form, then fold lightly into cream cheese mixture.

- Line base of 21-cm (8¹/₂-in) round springform cake tin with greaseproof paper. Grease paper and set aside.

- Cream butter and icing sugar until light and fluffy. Add vanilla essence. Beat in egg yolks one at a time, followed by egg white. Fold in sifted flour alternately with water. If necessary, add a little more water to achieve a dropping consistency.

- Pour batter into prepared tin. Even out surface. Bake in a preheated 175°C (350°F) oven for 25–30 minutes.

- Remove cake from oven. Spoon cheese layer over top of cake and spread evenly. Change oven to grill setting, then grill for about 10 minutes, or until cheese layer is firm to the touch. To prevent cheese layer from browning, cover with a flat tin lid.

- Remove cake from pan, allow to cool, then decorate with melted chocolate, if desired.

teacake  Makes one 20-cm (8-in) square cake

This teacake is similar to a fruit cake but the fruit is soaked in tea rather than brandy.

INGREDIENTS

Mixed dried fruit	250 g (9 oz), chopped
Mixed peel	120 g (4^1/$_5$ oz), chopped
Strong tea	125 ml (4 fl oz / ^{1}/$_2$ cup), cooled
Self-raising flour	240 g (8^1/$_2$ oz)
Ground cinnamon	1 tsp
Ground nutmeg	1 tsp
Butter	180 g (6^1/$_2$ oz)
Brown sugar	180 g (6^1/$_2$ oz)
Orange zest	grated from 1–2 oranges
Eggs	2

METHOD

• Start preparations for this cake a day ahead.

• Soak mixed fruit and peel in cooled strong tea and leave overnight.

• On baking day, line a 20-cm (8-in) square cake tin with greaseproof paper. Grease paper and set aside.

• Sift flour, cinnamon and nutmeg together. Set aside.

• Beat butter and sugar until light and creamy. Add orange zest, then beat in eggs one at a time. Add tea-soaked ingredients. Fold in sifted ingredients.

• Spread batter evenly in prepared cake tin. Bake in a preheated 175°C (350°F) oven for 50 minutes, or until a skewer inserted into the centre of cake comes out clean.

layer delight Makes one 20-cm (2.5-in) cake

Lacing the cake with rum gives it a lovely moist texture. The rum cream makes the cake extra special.

INGREDIENTS

Eggs	4, large
Castor (superfine) sugar	90 g (3 oz)
Vanilla essence	1 tsp
Self-raising flour	120 g (4^1/$_5$ oz), sifted
Corn oil	1 Tbsp
Milk	1 Tbsp
Rum	1–2 Tbsp

RUM CREAM

Seedless raisins	180 g (6^1/$_2$ oz)
Rum	4 Tbsp
Cold butter	250 g (9 oz), cut into small cubes
Icing sugar	150 g (5^1/$_3$ oz), sifted
Vanilla essence	1 tsp
Evaporated milk	1 can (170 g / 6 oz)

METHOD

• Prepare rum cream. Put raisins and 3 Tbsp rum in a small saucepan and bring to the boil over low heat. Remove from heat and leave to cool. Meanwhile, cream butter and sugar until light and creamy. Add vanilla essence, then beat in milk a little at a time. Beat in remaining rum. Divide mixture into two equal parts, then add raisins to one part. Set aside.

• Grease and flour two 20-cm (8-in) round cake tins.

• Whisk eggs, sugar and vanilla essence until light and fluffy. Sift in sifted flour and fold in quickly. Stir in corn oil and milk.

- Divide mixture equally between prepared tins. Bake in a preheated 190°C (375°F) oven for 15 minutes. Remove cakes from oven. Carefully spoon rum over cakes while cakes are still hot. Leave to cool on a wire rack.

- Sandwich rum cream with raisins between cakes. Coat and pipe top and sides of cake with remaining plain cream. Decorate as desired.

31

surprise cake Makes one 22-cm (9-in) round cake

The hidden pineapple layer offers the surprise in this cake.

INGREDIENTS

Butter	250 g (9 oz)
Castor (superfine) sugar	210 g (7^1/2 oz)
Vanilla essence	1 tsp
Lemon essence	1 tsp
Eggs	3, large
Self-raising flour	240 g (8^1/2 oz), sifted
Salt	1 pinch
Pineapple juice	4 Tbsp

PINEAPPLE LAYER

Butter	120 g (4^1/5 oz)
Brown sugar	115 g (4 oz)
Cornflakes	30 g (1 oz), crushed
Canned pineapple	1 can (565 g / 1 lb 4 oz), chopped
Desiccated coconut	30 g (1 oz)

METHOD

- Prepare pineapple layer. Cream butter and sugar. Add cornflakes, pineapple and coconut. Set aside.

- Line a 22-cm (9-in) round cake tin with greaseproof paper.

- Cream butter and sugar until light and creamy. Add essences, then beat in eggs one at a time. Fold in sifted flour. Add salt. Mix in 2 Tbsp pineapple juice.

- Spoon half the batter into prepared tin. Spoon half the topping over batter and spread evenly. Repeat with remaining batter and topping to form four layers. Bake in a preheated 175°C (350°F) oven for 40–45 minutes, or until cake is golden.

- Remove cake from oven and quickly spoon remaining 2 Tbsp pineapple juice over the top. Switch oven setting to grill, then return cake to oven for 10–12 minutes, or until topping turns light brown.

papaya sponge flan
Makes 21-cm (8¹/₂-in) flan

A refreshing dessert with a tropical flavour.

INGREDIENTS

Corn flour (cornstarch)	45 g (1¹/₂ oz)
Plain (all-purpose) flour	15 g (¹/₂ oz)
Baking powder	³/₄ tsp
Eggs	2
Castor (superfine) sugar	55 g (2 oz)
Lemon essence	¹/₂ tsp
Corn oil	1 Tbsp
Milk	2 tsp

PAPAYA LAYER

Ripe papaya	1, about 1–1.5 kg (2 lb 3 oz– 3 lb 4¹/₂ oz), peeled, seeded and cut into cubes
Orange zest	grated from 1 orange
Sugar	115 g (4 oz)
Lemon essence	1 tsp
Vanilla essence	1 tsp
Gelatine powder	2 Tbsp
Hot water	115 ml (4 fl oz), hot
Cream	1 small can (170 g / 6 oz)

METHOD

- Prepare papaya layer. Purée papaya and orange zest, then pour into a saucepan. Cover and cook over medium heat, stirring occasionally, until papaya purée is reduced to about 2¹/₂–3 cups. Remove from heat and set aside to cool. Stir in sugar and essences. Dissolve gelatine in hot water, then stir into cooled purée. Set aside. Whisk cream until firm peaks form, then fold lightly into papaya mixture.

- Grease a 21-cm (8¹/₂-cm) round springform cake tin.

- Sift corn flour, plain flour and baking powder together. Set aside.

- Whisk eggs, sugar and lemon essence until light and fluffy. Sift in sifted ingredients and fold in quickly and evenly. Stir in corn oil and milk.

- Pour batter into prepared tin. Bake in a preheated 190°C (375°F) oven for 10–15 minutes, or until cake springs back when lightly pressed with a finger.

- Pour papaya topping onto cooled cake and spread out evenly. Refrigerate until firm before removing cake from tin.

agar-agar flan delight
Makes one 20–22-cm (8–9-in) flan

Red food colouring gives this dessert a pretty pink hue. Use your favourite colour and decorate with other fruit as desired.

INGREDIENTS

Eggs	2, large
Castor (superfine) sugar	55 g (2 oz)
Vanilla essence	$^1/_2$ tsp
Self-raising flour	60 g (2$^1/_4$ oz)
Corn oil	$^1/_2$ Tbsp
Milk	$^1/_2$ Tbsp
Glacé cherries	2–3

AGAR-AGAR LAYER

Agar-agar strips	7 g ($^1/_3$ oz)
Water	340 ml (11$^1/_3$ fl oz)
Sugar	115 g (4 oz)
Vanilla essence	1 tsp
Red food colouring	2–3 drops
Egg white	1, large

METHOD

• Grease a 20–22-cm (8–9-in) flan tin.

• Whisk eggs, sugar and vanilla essence until thick and white. Sift in flour and fold in quickly. Stir in corn oil and milk.

• Bake in a preheated 190°C (375°F) oven for 15 minutes, or until golden. Let cake cool before turning out.

• Meanwhile prepare agar-agar layer. Wash agar-agar strips, then place into a saucepan with water. Bring to the boil and add sugar, stirring until sugar is dissolved. Remove from heat, then stir in vanilla essence and food colouring. Set aside. Beat egg white until just stiff. Strain agar-agar mixture into egg white, whisking all the time.

• Pour agar-agar onto cooled cake. Leave agar-agar cools, decorate with cherries. Refrigerate before serving.

cinnamon swiss roll
Makes one 27-cm (11-in) long Swiss roll

This soft Swiss roll cake is lightly flavoured with cinnamon and sweetened with honey. Replace the honey spread with whipped cream if desired.

INGREDIENTS

Corn flour (cornstarch)	60 g (2 1/4 oz)
Plain (all-purpose) flour	30 g (1 oz)
Baking powder	2 tsp
Ground cinnamon	2 tsp
Eggs	3
Castor (superfine) sugar	90 g (3 oz)
Vanilla essence	1 tsp

HONEY SPREAD

Butter	90 g (3 oz)
Honey	3 Tbsp

METHOD

- Line a Swiss roll tin, approximately 27 x 27-cm (11 x 11-in) with greaseproof paper. Grease paper and set aside.

- Sift corn flour, plain flour, baking powder and cinnamon together. Set aside.

- Whisk eggs until light and fluffy. Gradually beat in sugar. Add vanilla essence. Sift in sifted ingredients and fold in gently.

- Spread batter evenly in prepared tin. Bake in a preheated 190°C (375°F) oven for 12–15 minutes, or until cake is golden brown and springy to the touch. Turn cake out onto a clean tea towel. Peel off paper and trim off crisp edges. Gently roll up and leave to cool.

- Prepare honey spread. Beat butter until light. Add honey 1 Tbsp at a time.

- When cake is cool, gently unroll, then spread with honey spread and roll up again. Slice to serve.

coconut candy Makes about 30 squares

An all-time favourite with children, these coconut candy squares are not only pretty to look at, but tasty too!

INGREDIENTS

Grated skinned coconut	300 g (11 oz)
Sugar	565 g (1 lb 4 oz)
Evaporated milk	1 small can (170 g / 6 oz)
Butter	45 g (1 1/2 oz)
Vanilla essence	1 tsp
Green food colouring	a few drops

METHOD

• Put coconut, sugar and milk into a heavy saucepan. Stir continuously over low heat until sugar dissolves. Stir in butter, vanilla essence and food colouring. Keep stirring until mixture thickens. To test if ready, form a little of the mixture into a ball and drop into cold water. The mixture should hold its shape.

• Press suitably thickened mixture into a greased tray, approximately 15 x 18 cm (6 x 7-in). Cover with a plastic sheet, then use a rolling pin to even out surface. Leave to set and cool.

• When slightly cool, cut into squares. When completely cooled to room temperature, store in airtight containers.

rainbow wheels Makes 25–30 cookies

With their pretty colours, these cookies are a favourite with children. Vary the colours used
as desired.

INGREDIENTS

Self-raising flour	180 g (6$^1/_2$ oz)
Salt	1 pinch
Vegetable shortening	45 g (1$^1/_2$ oz)
Butter	45 g (1$^1/_2$ oz)
Castor (superfine) sugar	90 g (3 oz)
Vanilla essence	1 tsp
Egg	1, beaten
Green food colouring	a few drops
Orange food colouring	a few drops

METHOD

• Sift flour into a mixing bowl and sprinkle in salt. Rub in vegetable
  shortening and butter, then stir in sugar and vanilla essence. Bind
  mixture with beaten egg.

• Divide dough into 3 equal portions. Colour one portion green and
  one orange; leave the third uncoloured.

• Place each portion between lightly floured plastic sheets. Roll into
  15 × 22.5-cm (6 × 9-in) rectangles.

• Remove plastic sheets and stack dough rectangles together, with the
  uncoloured rectangle sandwiched in the middle. Roll up tightly from
  the long end. Place in the freezer for 10–15 minutes before cutting
  into 0.5-cm ($^1/_5$-in) thick slices.

• Arrange on greased trays, leaving enough room for cookies to expand.
  Bake in a preheated 175°C (350°F) oven for15–20 minutes until light
  golden. Remove and leave to cool on wire racks before storing in
  airtight jars.

watermelon jelly Serves 8–10

This dessert looks impressive, but can be prepared rather easily.

INGREDIENTS

Skinned coconut	1, grated
Agar-agar strips	50 g ($1^2/_3$ oz)
Water	900 ml (30 fl oz)
Sugar	340 g (12 oz)
Screwpine (*pandan*) leaves	3–4
Egg whites	7, large or 8, medium
Red food colouring	a few drops
Grass jelly (*chin chow*)	60 g ($2^1/_4$ oz), diced
Green food colouring	a few drops

METHOD

- Squeeze grated coconut, without adding water, to obtain coconut cream. Strain.

- Wash agar-agar strips. Put strips into a saucepan. Add water and sugar and bring to the boil. Stir to dissolve sugar and agar-agar.

- When sugar has dissolved, add screwpine leaves and coconut cream. Bring to the boil and remove from heat. Strain melted agar-agar into a measuring jug. There should be about 900 ml (30 fl oz) liquid.

- Whisk egg whites until just stiff. Whisk agar-agar liquid into egg whites until well combined. Pour into one 3-litre (96-fl oz / 12-cup), 21-cm ($8^1/_2$-in) bowl or two 18-cm (7-in) diameter soup bowls.

- When top of jelly sets, use a small knife to cut a circle on the surface, about 2.5 cm (1 in) from the edge. Add red colouring to the centre. Carefully mix with fingers, breaking lumps to get an even pink colour. Stir in black jelly to represent melon seeds. Refrigerate jelly until set.

- Remove jelly from refrigerator. Invert onto a dish. Rub green colouring onto curved surface to represent melon skin. Refrigerate and chill before serving.

raisin pinwheels Makes 16

These raisin pinwheels can be served piping hot from the oven or when cool.

INGREDIENTS

Sugar	3 tsp
Warm milk	5 Tbsp
Fresh yeast	30 g (1 oz)
Plain (all-purpose) flour	240 g (8$^1/_2$ oz), sifted
Salt	1 pinch
Butter	30 g (1 oz), softened, or 2 Tbsp corn oil
Egg	1, beaten
Raisins	60–90 g (2$^1/_4$–3 oz)

RUM SPREAD

Butter	60 g (2$^1/_4$ oz)
Icing sugar	90 g (3 oz), sifted
Rum	1 Tbsp

METHOD

• Dissolve sugar in milk. Add yeast and leave for 15 minutes until frothy.

• Sift flour into a bowl. Sprinkle in salt, then mix in butter or corn oil. Add yeast liquid and egg. Beat with a wooden spoon into a dough. Cover with a damp cloth and let stand for 1 hour until dough doubles in volume.

• Meanwhile, prepare rum spread. Cream butter and sugar, then stir in rum. Set aside.

• On a floured board, roll dough into a 20 × 25-cm (8 × 10-in) sheet. Fold evenly into three layers. Repeat to roll and fold dough, then halve dough. Roll each half into a 25 × 35-cm (10 × 14-in) rectangle.

• Spread dough with rum filling and sprinkle with raisins. Roll up Swiss-roll style, then cut into 2-cm (1-in) thick slices using a flat-bladed knife.

• Place on greased baking trays. Leave for 15 minutes to rise. Bake in an oven preheated to 200°C (400°F) for 12–15 minutes until golden. Transfer to a wire rack to cool.

sugar-coated doughnuts Makes 10

With a soft, melt-in-your-mouth texture, these doughnuts are a real treat! Omit the sugar-coating and dip into melted chocolate, if desired.

INGREDIENTS

Milk	105 ml (3²/₃ fl oz)
Water	85 ml (2¹/₂ fl oz)
Corn oil	¹/₂ Tbsp
Plain (all-purpose) flour	180 g (6¹/₂ oz)
Baking powder	1 tsp
Sugar	1 Tbsp
Salt	1 pinch
Egg	1, lightly beaten
Cooking oil for deep-frying	
Castor (superfine) sugar for coating	

METHOD

- Mix milk, water and corn oil together. Set aside.

- Sift flour and baking powder into a bowl. Stir in sugar and salt.

- Pour milk mixture into sifted ingredients. Mix with a spoon. Stir in beaten egg. Do not beat mixture.

- Spoon batter into doughnut maker and drop over hot oil. When doughnut rings float, turn them over immediately. Fry both sides until brown.

- Remove from oil and drain well. Coat with castor sugar.

grandma's pinwheels Makes 14

The sweet, warm aroma of these buns baking in the oven is hard to resist. Enjoy them freshly baked, although they also taste great when cool.

INGREDIENTS

Sugar	1 Tbsp
Warm milk	225 ml (7²/₃ fl oz)
Fresh yeast	2.5 x 5-cm (1 x 2-in) piece
Plain (all-purpose) flour	480 g (1 lb 1 oz), sifted
Salt	1 pinch
Lard or corn oil	1 cup
Eggs	4, beaten
Jam	quantity and flavour as desired
Chopped nuts (optional)	130 g (4½ oz)
Coarse white sugar for sprinkling	

METHOD

- Dissolve sugar in milk. Drop in yeast. Let stand for about 15 minutes until frothy.

- Sift flour into a bowl. Add salt and lard or corn oil. Mix by hand until ingredients are well combined. Add beaten eggs. Mix well. Stir in yeast liquid. Beat until smooth. Leave for about 1½ hours until dough doubles in volume.

- On a floured board, roll half the dough into a 30 x 35-cm (12 x 14-in) rectangle. Spread with jam. Sprinkle nuts, if used, over the top. Roll up Swiss-roll style. With a flour-coated knife, cut into 2-cm (1-in) thick rounds. Repeat with remaining dough.

- Arrange pinwheels on greased baking trays. Sprinkle coarse sugar over the top. Bake in an oven preheated to 175°C (350°F) for 25–30 minutes until golden.

cheese ropes Makes 42

These cheese ropes are easy to do and fun to make. Enjoy with tea or coffee.

INGREDIENTS

Butter	60 g (2^1/$_4$ oz)
Cream cheese	60 g (2^1/$_4$ oz), softened at room temperature
Egg	1
Salt	^{1}/$_2$ tsp
Ground white pepper	1 dash
Plain (all-purpose) flour	180 g (6^1/$_2$ oz)
Baking powder	1 tsp

METHOD

• Cream butter and cheese. Beat in egg. Add salt and pepper. Sift in flour and baking powder. Mix to form soft dough.

• On a lightly floured board, roll out dough. Cut 1-cm (^{1}/$_2$-in) wide strips.

• Shape each strip into a long and thin roll, then cut into 12.5-cm (5-in) lengths.

• Hold two lengths together, positioning one hand at each end. Twist by turning ends in opposite directions. Place on ungreased trays. Lightly press ends against tray to prevent them from becoming undone.

• Bake in a preheated 175°C (350°F) oven for 12–15 minutes, or until golden. Transfer to a wire rack to cool.

sardine rolls Makes 25

These mini sardine rolls are best served freshly baked. Plan to pop them into the oven just before your guests arrive.

INGREDIENTS

Pastry margarine	180 g (6^1/$_2$ oz), at room temperature
Kalamansi limes	2, squeezed for juice
Cold water	175 ml (6 fl oz)
Salt	^{1}/$_4$ tsp
Plain (all-purpose) flour	480 g (17 oz)
Baking powder	1^1/$_2$ tsp
Cold butter	90 g (3 oz), diced
Egg	1, beaten
Egg yolk	1, beaten
Evaporated milk	2 tsp

FILLING

Sardines	1 small can (150 g / 5^1/$_3$ oz), mashed
Cooking oil	1 Tbsp
Onion	1, peeled and finely chopped
Red and green chillies	2 each, seeded and finely sliced
Ground white pepper	1 dash
Limes	4, juice extracted

N O T E

Store unused dough in a sealed plastic bag and refrigerate or freeze. Frozen pastry will keep for up to 1 month. Thaw before using. Ready-rolled sheets of puff pastry is available from supermarkets. They are great when one is pressed for time.

METHOD

- Prepare filling. Heat oil in a wok and fry onion until fragrant. Add remaining ingredients and fry until quite dry. Set aside.

- Between large, clean plastic sheets, roll pastry margarine into a 20 x 15-cm (8 x 6-in) rectangle. Refrigerate.

- Combine lime juice, water and salt. Set aside.

- Sift flour and baking powder into a mixing bowl. Add cold butter and blend with pastry cutter or knife until mixture resembles breadcrumbs. Bind with egg and lime juice mixture using a wooden spoon. Turn contents out on a lightly floured board and knead into a soft but not sticky dough. Roll dough into a 40 x 15-cm (16 x 6-in) rectangular sheet.

- Remove plastic sheets from margarine. Place margarine in centre of dough rectangle, then fold ends of dough over to cover margarine. Seal edge.

- Roll dough parcel into a rectangle twice as long as it is wide. Fold rectangle into thirds widthways. Repeat process of rolling and folding twice. Halve dough. Reserve one portion for future use.

- On a lightly floured board, roll other half to 0.25 cm ($^1/_8$ in) thickness. Cut into 10 x 6-cm (4 x 2$^1/_2$-in) pieces. Put 1 tsp sardine filling on one short end of a pastry rectangle, then roll up. Seal edge with water. Repeat until ingredients are used up.

- Place rolls on ungreased cookie trays. Bake in a preheated 190°C (375°F) oven for 20–25 minutes, or until golden brown. In the meantime, make glaze by beating egg yolk and milk together.

- When done, remove rolls from oven and immediately brush with glaze.

cheese and bacon scones Makes 14

Enjoy these scones on their own, or slice and make a sandwich with tomato slices.

INGREDIENTS

Egg yolk	1, beaten
Water	1 tsp
Self-raising flour	240 g (8½ oz)
Margarine	60 g (2¼ oz)
Cheddar cheese	90 g (3 oz), grated
Bacon	90 g (3 oz), chopped
Milk	170 ml (6¾ fl oz)

METHOD

• Beat egg yolk and water together to make glaze. Set aside.

• Sift flour into a bowl. Lightly rub in margarine with fingers or blend with a pastry cutter. Stir in cheese and bacon. Mix with milk to form soft dough.

• On a lightly floured board, roll dough to 1–2-cm (½–1-in) thickness. Cut into 5–6 cm (2–2½-in) rounds. Place on lightly greased trays. Brush with glaze.

• Bake in a preheated 200°C (400°F) oven for 12–15 minutes, or until scones are golden brown. Serve.

savoury horns Makes 40

The unfilled and unglazed savoury horns will keep well in airtight containers for up to 2 weeks.

INGREDIENTS

Plain (all-purpose) flour	480 g (1 lb 1 oz)
Baking powder	2 tsp
Pastry margarine	240 g ($8^1/_2$ oz), at room temperature
Butter	75–90 g ($2^2/_3$–3 oz), softened at room temperature
Cold water	360–500 ml ($12^2/_3$–16 fl oz)
Egg yolk	1, beaten
Evaporated milk	2 tsp

FILLING

Cucumber	1, large, peeled, cored and diced
Ripe tomato	1, blanched, peeled and seeded
Crabmeat or chopped chicken	240 g ($8^1/_2$ oz), cooked
Thousand Island dressing	2–3 Tbsp
Ground white pepper	1 dash
Salt	$^1/_8$ tsp

METHOD

- Sift flour and baking powder into a bowl. Thinly slice pastry margarine into flour with a knife. Either rub in with fingers or blend with pastry cutter until mixture resembles fine breadcrumbs. Mix in butter with cold water. Bind well. Resulting dough should be soft but not too sticky. Cover dough with a dry cloth. Set aside for 15–30 minutes.

- On a floured board, roll dough to 1-cm ($^1/_2$-in) thickness. Fold into thirds. Repeat process of rolling and folding twice. Halve dough for easier handling. Roll each dough half to 0.25-cm ($^1/_8$-in) thickness. Cut into 30 x 1-cm (12 x $^1/_2$-in) pieces.

- Wind each piece around a cream horn tin, from point to wide end, overlapping slightly all the time. Place on ungreased trays, with exposed end of final round against tray's surface. Bake in a preheated 190°C (350°F) oven for 20 minutes, or until golden.

- In the meantime, make glaze by beating egg yolk and milk together. When done, remove horns from oven and immediately brush with glaze. Leave to cool.

- Prepare filling. Put crabmeat, cucumber and tomato into a bowl. Stir in salad dressing. Add pepper and salt to taste.

- Fill cooled horns with savoury filling and serve immediately.

siew mai Makes 40

These steamed meat dumplings are a popular type of dim sum.

INGREDIENTS

Wonton skins	40 sheets (7.5-cm (3-in) squares)
Cooked crab roe	1 Tbsp

FILLING

Minced prawns (shrimps)	240 g (8^1/$_2$ oz)
Minced fatty pork	240 g (8^1/$_2$ oz)
Cooked crabmeat	120 g (4^1/$_2$ oz)
Salt	1 tsp
Sesame seed oil	^{1}/$_2$ tsp
Ground white pepper	1 dash
Egg white	1
Corn flour (cornstarch)	1 ^{1}/$_2$ Tbsp
Corn oil	1 Tbsp
Dried Chinese mushrooms	2, soaked to soften, stems discarded and minced
Water chestnuts	3, peeled and minced
Spring onion (scallion)	1, thinly sliced

METHOD

• Prepare filling. Combine prawns, pork and crabmeat. Mix with salt, sesame seed oil, pepper and egg white. Stir in corn flour and corn oil. Beat mixture with a spoon. Mix in mushrooms, water chestnuts and spring onion. Refrigerate for 1 hour.

• Cut wonton skins into 7.5-cm (3-in) rounds with round cutter. Put 2 tsp filling in the centre of each skin. Gather edges of skin and smooth toward the top, letting it pleat naturally.

• Place wontons in greased bamboo baskets. Decorate tops with crab roe and steam for 12 minutes.

curry buns <small>Makes 24</small>

These curry buns are great for breakfast or as a snack. To reheat, use a toaster oven.

INGREDIENTS

Warm water	225 ml (7^2/$_3$ fl oz)
Milk	225 ml (7^2/$_3$ fl oz)
Sugar	2 Tbsp
Fresh yeast	30 g (1 oz)
Plain (all-purpose) flour	720 g (25^2/$_5$ oz)
Salt	1^1/$_2$ tsp
Butter	90 g (3 oz), softened at room temperature
Egg yolk	1, beaten
Evaporated milk	2 tsp

CURRY FILLING

Chicken, beef or pork	240 g (8^1/$_2$ oz), cut into small cubes
Curry powder	2 Tbsp
Cooking oil	2 Tbsp
Onions	2, diced or processed
Potatoes	2, medium, peeled and cut into small cubes
Salt	1 tsp

METHOD

• Mix half the warm water and milk. Set aside.

• Dissolve sugar in remaining warm water. Drop in yeast. Let stand for about 15 minutes until frothy.

• Sift flour into a mixing bowl. Add salt. Stir butter into flour. Add diluted milk and yeast liquid. Bind with a wooden spoon.

• On a lightly floured board, knead dough until crack-free. Return dough to bowl. Cover with damp cloth. Leave for about 1^1/$_2$ hours until dough doubles in volume. Punch dough down and let rise again.

- Meanwhile, prepare filling. Season meat with curry powder. Set aside. Heat oil in a wok and lightly brown onions. Add potatoes and cook until soft, adding some water to prevent burning. Add meat and stir-fry until cooked. Season with salt. Fry filling until dry. Dish out and set aside to cool.

- On a floured board, knead dough. Form into a long roll. Cut into 24 even-size pieces and shape into balls. Flatten balls and roll into rounds.

- Put a teaspoonful of filling in the centre of each round. Bring edges over filling and seal. Reshape parcels into smooth balls. Place well apart on greased trays. Leave to rise for 10–15 minutes.

- Bake in a preheated 200°C (400°F) oven for 15–20 minutes until golden brown.

- In the meantime, make glaze by beating egg yolk and evaporated milk together. Remove buns from oven and immediately brush with glaze.

savoury pancakes Makes about 12

Like breakfast pancakes, these savoury pancakes are best served fresh from the pan.

INGREDIENTS

Cooking oil	3 Tbsp
Shallots	3, peeled and sliced
Dried prawns (shrimps)	75 g (2½ oz), soaked to soften and minced
Plain (all-purpose) flour	300 g (11 oz)
Water	450 ml (15 fl oz)
Salt	¼ tsp
Ground white pepper	¼ tsp
Spring onions (scallions)	2–3, finely sliced

METHOD

- Heat oil in a non-stick pan. Fry shallots until light brown and crisp. Drain and set aside.

- Using the same wok, fry dried prawns over low heat until fragrant and crisp. Drain and set aside. Drain oil and reserve for frying pancakes later.

- Sift flour into a bowl. Stir in water to make smooth, runny batter. Strain batter if lumpy. Stir in salt, pepper and spring onions. Mix in fried shallots and prawns.

- Lightly grease a clean non-stick frying pan. Pour in a ladleful of batter. When batter is set and pancake is lightly brown on underside, flip pancake over and fry other side until lightly brown. Remove and leave to cool. Repeat to make more pancakes until batter is used up. Makes about 12.

- Roll pancakes up. Serve with chilli sauce of choice, or refer to recipe on page 70 to make your own.

char siew pau Makes 32

These buns are filled with a grilled meat filling. Use store-bought grilled meat if pressed for time.

INGREDIENTS

BUN (PAU)

Sugar	115 g (4 oz)
Lukewarm water	340 ml (11½ fl oz)
Fresh yeast	30 g (1 oz)
Plain (all-purpose) flour	675 g (1 lb 7½ oz)
Baking powder	½ Tbsp
Bicarbonate of soda	⅓ tsp
Salt	1 tsp
Corn oil	1 Tbsp

CHAR SIEW FILLING

Streaky pork or skinless chicken	600 g (1 lb 5½ oz)
Salt	2 tsp
Sugar	3 Tbsp
Light soy sauce	1 Tbsp
Dark soy sauce	½ tsp
Red food colouring	a few drops
Water	450 ml
Oyster sauce	2 tsp
Sesame seed oil	½ tsp
Corn flour (cornstarch)	2 tsp
Coriander leaves (cilantro)	1 sprig, chopped

METHOD

- Prepare filling. Pat meat dry with a tea towel. Cut 2.5-cm (1-in) strips. Season with salt, sugar, and soy sauces. Add colouring and leave for at least 2 hours, or overnight in the refrigerator.

- Place meat on a wire rack. Oven grill with a pan of water on the bottom shelf. Turn meat occasionally until cooked. Leave to cool before dicing. Reserve gravy.

- Combine 4 Tbsp gravy, oyster sauce, sesame seed oil and corn flour in a wok. Bring to the boil, then stir in diced meat and coriander. Dish out. Leave to cool.

- Prepare bun. Dissolve sugar in lukewarm water, then add yeast. Let stand for 10–15 minutes until frothy. Sift powdered ingredients into a bowl. Add salt. Gradually pour in corn oil and yeast liquid, stirring with a wooden spoon. When mixture becomes too difficult for the spoon, use hands to form firm dough. On a lightly floured board, knead dough for at least 10 minutes. Sprinkle flour occasionally to prevent dough from sticking to board.

- Return dough to bowl. Cover with a damp cloth. Leave for about 1 1/2 hours until dough doubles in volume. Punch dough down and let rise again for 20–30 minutes.

- On a lightly floured board, knead dough until smooth. Form two rolls, each 4 cm (1 1/2-in) in diameter. Cut into 2-cm (1-in) wide pieces. Flatten each piece with a roller. Put 1 tsp filling in the centre of each piece. Lift edge from one side and form pleats in one direction. Twist pleats together at the very top to seal bun.

- Place buns on rounds of greaseproof paper. Arrange well apart in bamboo baskets. Bring water in steamer to the boil over high heat. Steam buns for 12 minutes.

fried wontons Makes 60

These meat dumplings can also be served boiled in soup. Omit the last step and cook in meat or seafood stock.

INGREDIENTS

Wonton skins	60 sheets (7.5-cm (3-in) squares)
Egg white	1, beaten
Cooking oil for deep-frying	

FILLING

Prawns (shrimps)	120 g (4$^1/_2$ oz), small–medium
Egg white	$^1/_2$
Light soy sauce	1 tsp
Sugar	$^1/_2$ tsp
Salt	1 pinch
Ground white pepper	1 dash
Spring onion (scallion)	1, finely sliced
Coriander leaves (cilantro)	1 sprig, chopped

METHOD

- Prepare filling. Peel and wash prawns. Dry with a tea towel. Cut each prawn into 2–3 pieces. Season prawns with egg white, light soy sauce, sugar, salt and pepper for at least 30 minutes. Mix in spring onion and coriander.

- Place a wonton skin on a flat work surface, with a corner facing you. Put a few prawn pieces on wonton skin near this corner, then fold corner over prawns to meet centre of wonton skin. Roll wonton skin up halfway and lift both ends of rolled section up. Stick together using beaten egg white.

- Heat oil in a wok and deep-fry until golden. Remove and drain well. Serve hot with chilli sauce of choice or refer to recipe on page 70 to make your own.

prawn balls Makes about 50

These are great as finger food. Insert a bamboo fork into each one to make prawn ball lollipops.

INGREDIENTS

Prawns (shrimps)	600 g (1 lb 5$^1/_3$ oz), small–medium
Light soy sauce	2 tsp
Sesame seed oil	1 tsp
Salt	$^1/_2$ tsp
Sugar	$^1/_2$ tsp
Ground white pepper	1 dash
Egg white	$^1/_2$
Corn flour (cornstarch)	1 tsp
Spring onions (scallions)	2, finely sliced
Coriander leaves (cilantro)	1 sprig, finely sliced
Water chestnuts	4, peeled and minced
Day-old sliced white bread	600 g (1 lb 5$^1/_3$ oz), cut into very small cubes
Cooking oil for deep-frying	

CHILLI SAUCE

Red chillies	12, large and seeded
Garlic	3 cloves, peeled
Water	225 ml (8 fl oz)
Tomato sauce	2 Tbsp
Vinegar	$^1/_2$ Tbsp
Sugar	$^1/_2$ Tbsp
Salt	$^1/_4$ tsp
Cooking oil	1 Tbsp

METHOD

- Peel and wash prawns. Dry with a tea towel, then mince to a fine paste. Season with soy sauce, sesame seed oil, salt, sugar, pepper, egg white and corn flour. Stir in spring onions, coriander and water chestnuts. Refrigerate for at least 30 minutes.

- Meanwhile, prepare chilli sauce. Blend (process) chillies, garlic and water into a fine paste. Transfer to a small saucepan. Add remaining ingredients and bring to the boil. Remove from heat and leave to cool. Store in a glass jar at room temperature.

- Drop teaspoonfuls of chilled prawn mixture onto bread cubes and roll to coat well.

- Heat oil for deep-frying and deep-fry balls over low heat until golden. Remove and drain well. Serve with chilli sauce.

kuih pie tee Makes about 38

A Peranakan or Straits Chinese snack, these little filled cups make fun party finger food. Allow your guests to spoon the filling into the shells for themselves.

INGREDIENTS

PIE TEE CUPS

Plain (all-purpose) flour	90 g (3 oz)
Rice flour	1 Tbsp
Salt	$1/4$ tsp
Egg	1, beaten
Water	170 ml (6 fl oz)
Cooking oil for deep-frying	

FILLING

Cooking oil	3 Tbsp
Garlic	4 cloves, peeled and minced
Turnip	450 g (1 lb), peeled, finely shredded and squeezed of some excess water
Chicken or pork	240 g ($8^1/2$ oz), diced
Peeled prawns (shrimps)	240 g ($8^1/2$ oz), diced
Salt	1 tsp
Ground white pepper	$1/4$ tsp
Five-spice powder	$1/4$ tsp
Crabmeat	90 g (3 oz)
Chinese lettuce	1 head, torn into small pieces
Crisp-fried shallots	
Coriander leaves (cilantro)	

METHOD

- Prepare pie tee cups. Sift plain and rice flours into a small bowl. Add salt and stir in egg. Mix with water into a smooth, runny batter. Strain batter if lumpy.

- Heat oil for deep-frying in a deep pan. Warm pie tee mould in hot oil for 1 minute, then dip into batter and into hot oil. Fry until cup is golden. Loosen cup from mould, then remove from oil and drain well. Repeat until batter is used up. When cool, store in airtight containers until required.

- Prepare filling. Heat oil in a wok and lightly brown garlic. Add turnip and stir-fry lightly, then add chicken or pork and prawns. Season with salt, pepper and five-spice powder. Stir in crabmeat. Lower heat and simmer until quite dry. Dish out and set aside to cool.

- Just before serving, line pie tee cups with lettuce. Spoon 2 tsp filling into each cup. Garnish with crisp-fried shallots and coriander leaves. Serve with chilli sauce of choice or refer to recipe on page 70.

kuih nagasari Makes 16

A sort of banana pudding, this sweet dessert yields the best results when made with the small *raja* variety of bananas.

INGREDIENTS

Rice flour	240 g (8$\frac{1}{2}$ oz)
Water	500 ml (16 fl oz / 2 cups)
Coconut milk	875 ml (30$\frac{4}{5}$ fl oz), obtained from squeezing 1 grated coconut mixed with sufficient water
Screwpine (*pandan*) leaves	2, knotted
Salt	$\frac{1}{2}$ tsp
Banana leaves	16, cut into 18 x 15-cm (7 x 6-in) pieces, scalded
Small ripe bananas (*raja* variety)	8, peeled and halved lengthways

METHOD

- Sift rice flour into a bowl. Add water and mix until smooth.

- Into a saucepan, put coconut milk, screwpine leaves and salt. Bring to a slow boil. Add rice flour batter and stir with a wooden spoon for about 5 minutes, or until mixture becomes a smooth paste. Remove from heat.

- Onto the centre of each banana leaf, place a dessertspoonful of cooked mixture. Fold over one side of banana leaf to flatten and shape mixture into a small rectangle. Unfold leaf, top with a banana half and cover with another spoonful of cooked mixture. Fold banana leaf in thirds lengthways, overlapping to cover mixture. Then, fold two short ends under so parcel's weight rests on them. Repeat until ingredients are used up.

- Steam parcels for 20 minutes. Serve hot or cold.

kuih serimuka Makes one 25–27-cm (10–11-in) round cake

This popular Nyonya dessert has a layer of screwpine-flavoured custard over lightly salted glutinous rice.

INGREDIENTS

TOP LAYER

Small coconut	1, grated
Water	250 ml (8 fl oz / 1 cup)
Eggs	4
Sugar	180 g (6^1/$_2$ oz)
Plain (all-purpose) flour	90 g (3 oz)
Tapioca flour	30 g (1 oz)
Screwpine (*pandan*) juice	4 Tbsp (from pounding and squeezing screwpine leaves)
Green food colouring	a few drops
Vanilla essence	^{1}/$_2$ tsp

BOTTOM LAYER

Skinned coconut	^{1}/$_2$, grated
Water	340 ml (11^1/$_2$ fl oz)
Glutinous rice	450 g (1 lb)
Salt	1^1/$_4$ tsp

METHOD

• Prepare top layer. Blend grated coconut with water. Squeeze and strain to obtain 375 ml (12 fl oz / ^{1}/$_2$ cups) thick coconut milk.

• Stir eggs and sugar together in a bowl. Do not beat. Sift in plain and tapioca flours. Mix well. Gradually pour in coconut milk, screwpine juice, colouring and essence. Strain to remove lumps. Set top layer aside.

• Prepare bottom layer. Combine coconut and water, then squeeze to obtain coconut milk. Strain.

- Wash glutinous rice and place into a 25–27-cm (10–11-in) round pan. Pour in enough coconut milk to cover rice, then stir in salt. Place in a steamer and steam for 20–25 minutes, until rice is cooked. Press rice firmly down with the back of a spoon.

- Pour top layer over rice and steam for 20 minutes over medium heat. Leave to cool. Slice to serve.